T0293905

THE BUSES OF EAST SCOTLAND

RICHARD WALTER

AMBERLEY

Front cover: Borders Buses ADL E40D Enviro400 MMC 11902 (SK19 ELW), pictured leaving Galashiels on the X62 service to Peebles. The cycle-friendly bus has space to carry four bikes per vehicle.

Rear cover: Lothian Country 9201 (SB19 GKE) is one of eight Plaxton Leopard Interurban bodied Volvo B8Rs purchased for Green Arrow express services and is seen at the Linlithgow terminus of service EX2. The high spec vehicles feature an impressive nearside disabled ramp entrance for wheelchair users.

First published 2020

Amberley Publishing
The Hill, Stroud
Gloucestershire, GL5 4EP

www.amberley-books.com

Copyright © Richard Walter, 2020

The right of Richard Walter to be identified as the Author of this work has been asserted in accordance with the Copyright, Designs and Patents Act 1988.

ISBN 978 1 4456 9639 3 (print)
ISBN 978 1 4456 9640 9 (ebook)

British Library Cataloguing in Publication Data.
A catalogue record for this book is available from the British Library.

Origination by Amberley Publishing.
Printed in the UK.

Contents

Introduction

If you mention Scotland to visitors arriving in the UK, their usual reaction is to identify Loch Ness, Ben Nevis and the Highlands as their must-see destinations. However, the east of Scotland has much to boast in the way of impressive attractions and breath-taking scenery.

There are, of course, the larger cities such as Edinburgh, Aberdeen and Dundee, but also a wide range of smaller places from the Scottish Borders to Fife, offering stunning countryside and seaside settings. And there is plenty to see by bus. Castles, palaces, Holyrood – home of the Scottish Parliament – Forth bridges, festivals – including the world famous Edinburgh International Festival Fringe and Tattoo – seabird centres, harbours, mining, flight and other museums and art galleries, the Royal Yacht *Britannia* and, not forgetting, a number of world-renowned whisky distilleries.

Public transport is very varied and colourful in this region. In addition to the large, well-known companies such as Stagecoach, Firstbus, Scottish Citylink, National Express and Borders Buses – part of West Coast Motors (Craig of Campbeltown Group) – there is the family of Lothian Buses which covers Edinburgh, East Lothian, Midlothian and West Lothian and a host of well-known smaller operators such as Prentice of Haddington, Eve of Dunbar, Rennies, E&M Horsburgh, Moffat & Williamson, Prentice Westwood and Bay Travel. Some routes and areas have changed ownership in recent years and more change is likely, including further integration with trains and trams.

For this book I have selected photographs which I hope will give a good representation of some of the many companies, vehicle types and livery styles, shown in the spectacular rural and city locations that they serve, at the time of writing.

I explore the innovative ideas that have been tried out, including the introduction of autonomous buses in Fife, facilities for taking your bike on board, longer and larger-capacity tri-axle buses and coaches, open top tours of the more rural areas of east Scotland and the Scottish Borders, contactless payment, Wi-Fi and USB charging and localised route branding. And there's a look at some of the demonstrators that have been trialled in recent years.

The design of buses is changing and developing all the time, as are the providers of bus and coach services. Whilst preparing this book, Wrightbus went into administration, being saved at the very last moment. It remains to be seen how future orders will be affected, with ADL in Falkirk and Scarborough already manufacturing many of the single and double-deck buses in the east of Scotland. Interesting times are ahead.

My thanks go to Andrew Chalmers, Chris Cuthill, Gordon Stirling and Alistair Train for their photographic contributions and assistance. All are credited for their particular work. The uncredited pictures were taken by me.

Aberdeen

The attractive and eye-catching First Aberdeen Platinum livery on Wright Eclipse Gemini-bodied Volvo B9TL 37640 (SV08 FXY), pictured on Broad Street, Aberdeen, on service 19 to Tillydrone.

First Aberdeen black and gold version of the Platinum livery, as applied to ADL Enviro200 MMC 67085 (SN65 ZGA). The bus is seen on route X27 in Broad Street, en route to Guild Street, but branded for route 13.

New to First Glasgow, but now transferred to First Aberdeen, is ADL Trident Enviro500 tri axle 38206 (SN09 CBU), photographed at the Robert Gordon University terminus on route 1 to Danestone. The bus has prominent vinyls for contactless payments on board.

First Aberdeen Thistleline branding on Wright Streetlite Max 63217 (SN14 FEP), which carries the banner 'Walker Road School – Voytek the Brace Bear' and is seen on service 3 to Cove and Charleston via Union Square.

For some years now, Aberdeen has been taking part in fuel cell trials with buses in a special livery split between Stagecoach Bluebird and First Aberdeen. Van Hool A330 Hydrogen Fuel Cell 64496 (SV14 FZD) is one of the four examples with First and is seen on service X27 to Heliport.

Brought in during 2015 to upgrade their Buchan Express routes, Stagecoach Bluebird 54246 (YX65 ZKF) is one of a number of Plaxton Elite Volvo B11RTs caught on service 67 from Peterhead and Fraserburgh. It was photographed heading towards Aberdeen bus station.

Attractive JET-liveried Stagecoach Bluebird ADL Enviro400 MMC 10533 (SN16 OMX), passing Marischal College on Broad Street on its way in from Aberdeen airport.

Seen in special hybrid livery is Stagecoach Bluebird ADL Enviro350H 29010 (SV12 DAO), which also carries Hospital Direct branding for service 59 to Northfield.

Stagecoach Bluebird ADL Enviro400 MMC 11167 (SK19 EKL), on service 35 to Oldmeldrum with the distinctive branding for 'Get a Bonnie View Fae the Top Deck'. You can almost hear the Doric dialect.

Slightly off its usual branded service 35 is Stagecoach Bluebird ADL Enviro400 MMC 11175 (SK19 EKW), heading along Union Street on service 202.

The Scottish Borders

Borders Buses Low Carbon Optare Solo 11503 (YJ15 AAX), previously new to Perrymans in May 2015, is seen on service 253 (Edinburgh–Berwick-upon-Tweed) before the company became part of the West Coast Motors group during 2016. It was photographed approaching Innerwick with Torness power station in the background. (Alistair Train)

Borders Buses MCV Evolution-bodied Mercedez Benz OC500LE 11209 (AE12 AZC) on service 67 to Berwick, leaving Galashiels. The bus was also new to Perrymans.

Another former Perrymans transfer to the Borders Buses fleet was Optare Versa 11307 (YA13 AEJ), captured on Old Dalkeith Road on service 52 to Lauder.

Borders Buses Optare MetroCity 11709 (SN17 MUA) on the busy service X62 to Peebles at Lady Road, Edinburgh.

Borders Buses Optare MetroCity 11615 (YJ66 AEA) – again new to Perrymans in November 2016 – on service 253 to Berwick-upon-Tweed at the Jewel, Edinburgh.

Bought from Whitelaw's of Stonehouse in 2017 by Borders Buses and seen here at Cameron Toll is Wright Eclipse-bodied Volvo B7RLE 11226 (BF12 KWW), heading on an X62 to Peebles.

Delivered new to Borders Buses is Plaxton Leopard-bodied Volvo B8R 11729 (YX67 URP), seen leaving Galashiels on service X95 to Hawick.

New to Parks of Hamilton, and originally registered HSK 660, is Borders Buses Plaxton Elite Volvo B9R 11231 (SB12 WDF), passing Cameron Toll on an X62 to Peebles.

Borders Buses ADL Enviro400 MMC 11621 (YN66 BBZ) started its life as bus 777 with Reading Buses before joining the Craig of Campbelltown Group in October 2016. It was pictured leaving Galashiels on service X62 to Melrose.

Pictured at Straiton on service X62 to Peebles, former demonstrator Scania N280UD ADL EnviroMMC 11622 (YN16 CFU), now with Borders Buses, was given this distinctive tartan vinyl wrapround for the My Name's Doddie Foundation motor neuron disease fundraising campaign. Doddie Weir OBE is one of rugby's most recognisable personalities, having earned sixty-one caps for Scotland during his career.

Borders Buses ADL Enviro400 MMC 11801 (YX67 UZB), on the X62 to Melrose, leaving Galashiels Transport Interchange, still in the smart demonstration livery that it wore from new. Borders Buses bought the vehicle following trialling it in service.

Borders Buses ADL Enviro400 MMC 11801 (YX67 UZB) was duly repainted into the most up-to-date fleet colours and was captured undertaking shuttle duties for a golf event in North Berwick.

Borders Buses have been taking delivery of bike-friendly buses during 2019 and 2020. ADL E40D Enviro400 MMC 11901 (SK19 ELV) is seen on the first route to benefit from the bike spaces – the X62 – heading to Peebles from Edinburgh via Cameron Toll.

Borders Buses ADL E40D Enviro400 MMC 11903 (SK19 ELX) on an X62 leaving Galashiels. As well as spaces for bikes, onboard features include free WiFi, contactless payment, comfortable seating and tables, wireless and USB charging points and device friendly seat backs.

Another Borders Buses ADL E40D Enviro400 MMC 11902 (SK19 ELW), pictured leaving Galashiels on the X62 to Peebles. The company have an app where it is possible to track the respective bike-friendly buses to see what runnings they are on. Initially the intention was to feature two bikes per vehicle but based on passenger feedback, space was quickly expanded to carry four.

Borders Buses Optare MetroCity 11727 (YJ17 FZC) has received the newer style of livery, as shown here as it leaves the Transport Interchange at Galashiels on an X95 to Hawick.

Borders Buses ADL Enviro200 11715 (YY17 GSU) at Midlothian Community Hospital on route 339 to Gorebridge. This service used to be provided by Lothian Buses service 39. When East Coast Buses took over the route as the 139, it terminated at the hospital with Borders Buses service 339 covering the section of route to Gorebridge.

Recent deliveries to Borders Buses include the first ten of twenty bike-friendly ADL Enviro200 MMCs, split between Galashiels and Berwick depots. Last of the first batch, 11922 (SN69 ZNO) is seen approaching Edinburgh bus station on loan to Galashiels, briefly after delivery, for use on Berwick route 253. The bus initially did not carry route branding.

Fully branded Borders Buses ADL E40D Enviro400 MMC 11913 (SN69 ZNC) heads into Edinburgh on service 253 to Edinburgh via the Jewel, Edinburgh.

Borders Buses ADL E40D Enviro400 MMC 11917 (SN69 ZNH) setting out from Galashiels on service X95 with suitable route branding and information about bike spaces.

A number of demonstrators have been trialled by Borders Buses since the company was formed. ADL Enviro200 MMC 41901 (YX19 OWA) appeared on service X62 to Peebles and resulted in a subsequent sizeable order for similar vehicles. The bus was pictured at Darnick Vale on the outskirts of Melrose. (Chris Cuthill)

This double-deck Borders Buses demonstrator, SN66 WLK, also spent some time on the X62 to Peebles. The bus is an ADL Enviro400 City and ended up being bought by Courtney Buses and painted in Milton Park livery for use in Reading.

The most unusual visitor to the Borders Buses fleet was an Irizar i4 Hybrid coach demonstrator. In this photo, YN67 VCZ is seen on Old Dalkeith Road nearing the Royal Infirmary of Edinburgh on service X95.

Another view of Borders Buses Irizar i4 Hybrid coach demonstrator YN67 VCZ, seen by Shawfair, leaving Edinburgh on the X95 to Newtongrange.

Borders Buses also trialled this Citaro Mercedes demonstrator on the X95. BT66 TZE was photographed on layover at Edinburgh bus station.

Looking very distinctive in a bright orange and white livery is Borders Buses Optare MetroCity demonstrator XFE 41706 (YJ17 FXE), picking up passengers on North Bridge.

Borders Buses provided a short-lived open-top City Sightseeing tour of the Scottish Borders in 2018 using Alexander PS-bodied Volvo B10M 19702 (M800 WCM). This bus started life in 1997 with Greater Manchester South as closed top 928 (R928 XVM). It passed to Stagecoach as 20928 before joining Quantock Motor Services of Bishops Lydeard in Taunton. On conversion to open-top, it operated a sightseeing tour of Oban before transferring to Borders Buses. (Alistair Train)

Borders Buses Optare Solo 10701 (MX07 NTU) showing a dedicated livery for service 477 from Berwick to Holy Island. (Alistair Train)

First Midland Bluebird Wright Eclipse-bodied Scania 65745 (SN55 JVK), in special vinyls promoting the Borders Railway, passes by Tweedbank Loch on service 72 to Borders General Hospital. (Chris Cuthill)

Scottish Borders Council operated Mellor-bodied Iveco SN11 FDG, also in Borders Railway vinyls, on the 964 Borders Weaver service. Pictured at Tweedbank station. (Alistair Train)

CitylinkAIR – Edinburgh Airport to Glasgow Buchanan Bus Station

West Coast Motors and Scottish Citylink operate a very busy AIR service between Edinburgh Airport and Glasgow bus station. One of the early vehicles used on the service was Irizar i6 Scania K410EB6 YT13 YUD, which originally carried a split livery of West Coast Motors red and cream at the front and Citylink yellow and blue at the rear.

Irizar i6 Scania K410EB6 YS16 LMM was new to Craig of Campbeltown as 11607 in July 2016. It is seen in an attractive dedicated livery leaving Glasgow Buchanan bus station on the Scottish Citylink AIR service to Edinburgh Airport.

At the end of 2019, West Coast Motors and Scottish Citylink introduced new high-spec ADL Plaxton Panoramas on their AIR services. YX69 LHH arrives at the terminal point at Edinburgh Airport on its first day in service in October 2019.

ADL Plaxton Panorama YX69 LHK leaving Edinburgh Airport bound for Glasgow Buchanan Bus Station in its attractive three-tone blue livery.

Dundee

Tayside Public Transport Company Limited (trading as Xplore Dundee) is a wholly owned subsidiary of National Express Group plc. National Express Xplore Dundee 5425 (SP13 BSU) is an ADL Enviro400, new in April 2000. It carries the green hybrid version of the then corporate livery. Named *Hannah Miley*, it is pictured on service 10 to Barnhill.

National Express Xplore Dundee Wright Eclipse Gemini Volvo B7TL 4686 (BX54 XTD), with Christmas vinyls, on service 5 to Ninewells Hospital.

New to West Midlands Travel in January 2017, and now with National Express Xplore Dundee, is Wright Eclipse Urban-bodied Volvo B7RLE 1775 (BX56 XCU), on branded service 32 to Fintry, showing off the initial green Xplore Dundee livery that many buses have been repainted into.

National Express Xplore Dundee ADL Enviro400 5428 (SP13 BSY) is another vehicle in the revised dark green livery on service 5. Pictured arriving at Ninewells Hospital.

National Express Xplore Dundee introduced fourteen new Emerald-branded buses in 2018. ADL Enviro400 MMC 6687 (SK68 LZR), in its smart new application of lighter shades of green, attracted much attention at the 2018 Euro Bus Expo at the National Exhibition Centre in Birmingham.

A few weeks later, National Express Xplore Dundee ADL Enviro400 MMC 6687 (SK68 LZR) is seen back in Dundee and in service on route 22 to Ninewells.

Another National Express Xplore Dundee ADL Enviro400 MMC, 6698 (SK68 MBX), on service 22 with route branding, arrives at Ninewells Hospital.

National Express West Midlands ADL Enviro400 4905 (BX13 JWE) was loaned to National Express Xplore Dundee for Dundee Pride 2019 and is seen participating at the Bus Driver of the Year event in Blackpool that year. (Andrew Chalmers)

National Express Xplore Dundee Wright StreetLite 434 (SN65 OMD), named *Ryan*, in a special vinyled livery for City Circle 360.

Originally new to Kings Ferry in Kent, in October 2013, but now with National Express Xplore Dundee, is Caetano Levante Volvo B9R 452 (BF63 ZSX) – one of two similar vehicles operated on the X90 service between Dundee and Edinburgh Airport.

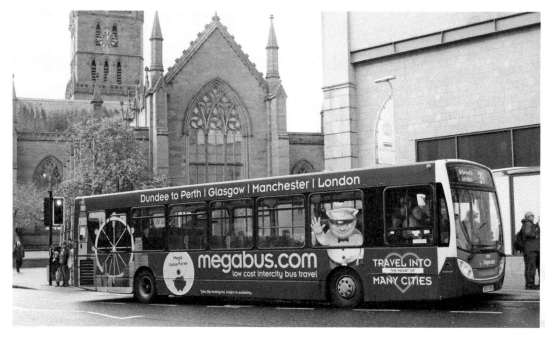

Stagecoach East Scotland ADL Enviro300 27530 (SP57 CPE) was new to Perth as a Goldline vehicle in 2007. It now carries Megabus advertising livery and was caught in Dundee city centre on service 39 to Arbroath.

Delivered to Stagecoach Fife/Strathtay in May 2015 is Volvo B5LH Enviro400 MMC 13054 (SA15 VTV), with Go Green Travel Tayway branding for service 73 to Ninewells Hospital.

Stagecoach Optare Versa 25269 (MX09 HJJ) loading up in Dundee on service 79A to Monikie, a small village in Angus.

Moffat & Williamson Mellor Strata Sprinter LM18 DZE, off service and seen approaching Ninewells Hospital.

Moffat & Williamson SP59 DCE is an Optare Solo M950, new to the fleet in September 2009. It was pictured on service 77B to Wormit.

Moffat & Williamson ADL Enviro400 MMC SN66 WHR in Dundee on tendered service 236 to Claverhouse. (Chris Cuthill)

East Lothian and Midlothian

Prentice of Haddington operate a number of eco-friendly ADL Envio200 buses that meet low carbon bus status as they produce 30 per cent less greenhouse gases than a standard bus. An example is SN66 WKV, pictured on service 108 to Fort Kinnaird.

Prentice of Haddington ADL Enviro200 YX14 RXC, operating service 118 at Wallyford Toll on its way to Longniddry.

Service 69 – a short route connecting Portobello and Willowbrae – used to be operated by Lothian Buses. The service is now run in conjunction with Prentice of Haddington, with Lothian tickets and passes being accepted. All-white ADL Enviro200 YN15 NJE approaches Kings Road.

New to the Prentice of Haddington fleet in October 2016 was Mercedes-Benz Sprinter 516CDi/ Mellor Strata DF66 PSX, on service 110 to Elphinstone at Tranent.

Prentice of Haddington operated ADL Enviro200 SN12 EHL for a while in a dedicated 'Supersonic Gannet' livery. Seen here on service 121 at the National Museum of Flight Scotland at East Fortune. (Alistair Train)

Another venture to attract tourists. Prentice of Haddington used ADL Enviro200 YX12 DHL on the 527 Midlothian Explorer service. It was pictured at the National Mining Museum in Newtongrange. The service no longer operates. (Alistair Train)

A few demonstration vehicles have spent time with Prentice of Haddington. ADL Enviro200 MMC YX18 KWV was photographed on service 108 to Haddington at the River Esk in Musselburgh.

Prentice of Haddington also trialled ADL Enviro200 MMC YX17 NLF, seen here on service 111 to Haddington leaving the Royal Infirmary of Edinburgh.

East Coast Buses operated a tour of East Lothian from North Berwick, during the summer of 2018, using two semi-open-top converted East Lancs-bodied Scania OminCity 94s which had been withdrawn from the Lothian Buses fleet. One of these was 20994 (SN57 DCE).

Another picture of East Coast Buses East Lancs-bodied Scania OminCity 94 20994 (SN57 DCE), passing the road to popular tourist attraction Tantallon Castle.

East Coast Buses Wright Eclipse Gemini-bodied Volvo B7TL 20938 (SN10 DKF) turns by the Mercat Cross in Pencaitland, near the terminus of the 113.

As with other parts of the UK, East Lothian has witnessed some extreme flooding in recent years. East Coast Buses Wright Eclipse Gemini-bodied Volvo B7TL 20943 (SN10 DKU) crosses a large puddle, following severe rain in Musselburgh, on a service 124 to Edinburgh.

East Coast Buses borrowed Lothian Buses Wright Eclipse Gemini-bodied Volvo B9TL 856 ((SN57 DFJ), named *Hamish* and given green tartan vinyls during a campaign for MacMillan Cancer Support Scotland). It is seen here at the Jewel, Edinburgh, on limited stop service X7 to Haddington.

East Coast Buses operate eight Wright Gemini 3-bodied Volvo B5TLs with extra comfortable leather seats. 20003 (SJ18 NFT) passes the Brunton Hall, Musselburgh, on the 124 service to North Berwick.

Originally purchased for service 124 prior to the introduction of higher capacity Volvo B5TLs, displaced East Coast Buses Wrightbus Eclipse Urban 3 Volvo B8RLE 10055 (SF17 VMC) was photographed on service 106 to Haddington from Fort Kinnaird.

East Coast Buses Wrightbus Eclipse Urban 3 Volvo B8RLE 10054 (SF17 VMA), seen when new on the 124 at Wallyford. These 13.2-m-long high-spec buses feature leather seats and have proved to be very popular with passengers and drivers.

East Coast Buses Wrightbus Eclipse Urban Volvo B7RLE 10198 (SN62 BUF), on Dalkeith local service 139 to Hardengreen, approaching the Tesco store. This is one of two Midlothian services operated by the company.

East Coast Buses Wrightbus Eclipse Urban Volvo B7RLE 10196 (SN62 BPV) leaves Musselburgh on the 140 service to Penicuik.

Eve of Dunbar's Slimline Optare Solo SR E27 (YD63 VEP) on the 121 to Haddington at North Berwick.

Eve of Dunbar's Optare Solo M960 E23 (YJ62 FZR) at Pencaitland on the 123 Gifford Circle. (Alistair Train)

Eve of Dunbar's Optare Solo M810SL E25 (T3 EVE), new to the fleet as YJ11 OHV, was pictured at Innerwick on Dunbar Rural Service 130. (Alistair Train)

The impressive Berwick Law can be seen behind Eve of Dunbar's Optare Solo E24 (YJ62 FZO) as it passes through Drem on service 121 to Haddington. (Alistair Train)

Edinburgh

Lothian Buses Edinburgh Bus Tours open-top Plaxton President-bodied Dennis Trident 2 219 (XIL 1481), on loan to East Coast Buses, running a duplicate 124 service from North Berwick to Edinburgh during the summer of 2017.

Lothian Buses Wrightbus Gemini 3-bodied Volvo B5TL 1054 (SJ18 NFE), at Bellevue, on service 8 to the Royal Infirmary of Edinburgh.

During 2018 and 2019, the hybrid Volvo 7900Hs have been refurbished and repainted into the current Lothian Buses fleet livery. Seen here is 31 (BG64 FXD), in Queensferry Street, on service 36 heading to Ocean Terminal.

During 2019, Lothian Buses trialled a VolvoB8R with MCV Evora bodywork from Central garage. Numbered 299 (BV19 LND) it is seen on service 24 to West Granton at Cameron Toll.

Climbing out of Edinburgh at Ferniehill with Arthur's Seat in the background is Wrightbus Gemini 2 bodied Volvo B9TL 421 (BN64 CSU) on service 7. The bus is one of a few that carried special wraparound advertising for Glenfiddich Experimental Series malt whisky.

Lothian Buses Wrightbus Eclipse Urban Volvo B7RLE 551 (SA15 VUB) has worn a number of Poppy Scotland liveries. It is seen in the 2019 version on service 44 at Wallyford on a cold autumn afternoon.

Lothian Buses Wrightbus Gemini-bodied Volvo B9TL 892 (SN08 BXE) on service 4 to Hillend at Oxgangs.

Lothian Buses Wrightbus Gemini 3-bodied Volvo B5TL 588 (SJ67 MHA) (originally new to the Skylink fleet), on service 35 to Riccarton, leaves Ocean Terminal.

Lothian Buses Wrightbus Gemini bodied Volvo B9TL 856 (SN57 DFJ) spent some time in a special green tartan vinyl wrap for the MacMillan Cancer Campaign (as seen in the East Lothian section of this book). In November 2019 it was transformed into this colourful promotion for Essential Edinburgh. The photo was taken at the leafy terminus of service 23 at Greenbank.

Purchased in 2017 for use from Central garage, Lothian Buses have six Wright StreetAir electric buses. 287 (SK67 FLF) is seen in the Queen's Park on the short journey of service 6 from the Scottish Parliament at Holyrood to Hanover Street.

Lothian Buses operate a number of converted-to-single-door refurbished former London Wright Gemini-bodied Volvo B9TLs. 1001 (LXZ 5383) was one of the first two that received treatment at Thorntons. The other refurbishments were completed by Wrightbus. 1001 was pictured on service 14 at Greendykes with Craigmillar Castle in the background. Since the photo was taken, new houses have been built which now obscure this view.

From the second batch of refurbished London Wright Gemini-bodied Volvo B9T1s, Lothian Buses 1146 (LX11 CVL) awaits time at the 45 terminus at Queen Margaret University, Musselburgh, before departing for the university campus at Riccarton on the other side of Edinburgh. All but one of the second batch retained their centre doors and all kept their original London registrations.

2019 saw the arrival of 100-seat tri-axle buses in Edinburgh. It also marked 100 years of buses in Edinburgh. Lothian Buses 1125 (SJ19 OZD) is on service 16 to Colinton and was photographed at Oxgangs. It was delivered in an all-white livery before picking up a special centenary livery.

Lothian Buses Alexander Dennis Enviro400 XLB bodied Volvo B8L 1125 (SJ19 OZD) is seen passing Ryan's Bar at the West End of Edinburgh in its full centenary livery on its way to the University of Edinburgh King's Buildings on service 41.

Lothian Buses Alexander Dennis Enviro400 XLB-bodied Volvo B8L 1113 (SJ19 OYR) heads towards Silverknowes on service 29. The photo clearly shows the length of these 100-seat buses. The 29 route heads out to Gorebridge in Midlothian in the other direction.

Long before the arrival of East Coast Buses, Lothian Buses operated into parts of East Lothian. Service 26 connects Clerwood with either Seton Sands or Tranent. Wrightbus Gemini 3-bodied Volvo B5TL 484 (SF17 VNV) heads along the coast towards Prestonpans, displaying one of a number of Edinburgh Zoo adverts. The entire batch of '17 plate buses based at Marine garage feature different zoo animals and birds, following a long association the company has had with the Royal Zoological Society of Scotland.

Lothian Buses Wrightbus Gemini 2 bodied Volvo B9TL 417 (BN64 CRX) promoting the Platinum Edition 2020 seventieth anniversary of the Royal Edinburgh Military Tattoo. The bus is on service 25 to Riccarton university campus and was photographed leaving the Restalrig area at the other end of the route.

Lothian Motorcoaches (through Lothian Buses) provide a term-time free shuttle bus for University of Edinburgh students. Refurbished Wrightbus Gemini-bodied Volvo B9TL 847 (MXZ 1757) was photographed leaving the King's Buildings terminus.

Lothian Buses Wright StreetAir electric bus 288 (SK67 FLG) is wrapped in dedicated Standard Life vinyls for shuttle bus service 61, which connects employees between offices at Canon Street, at the west end of Edinburgh, and Canonmills.

Bought as part of a number of second-hand acquisitions for Lothian Motorcoaches, Caetano-bodied Volvo B9R 9061 (FJ11 MMF) was garaged at Central depot during the summer of 2019 and operated seasonal route 913 to Fort William on behalf of Scottish Citylink. It is seen in the white livery it wore at Halbeath Park and Ride.

Lothian Buses Wrightbus Eclipse 2 Urban Volvo B7RLE 189 (SN13 BFP) was photographed on a spring morning on Old Dalkeith Road on the service 49 to Rosewell.

Lothian Buses all-white Wrightbus Eclipse Urban Volvo B7RLE 115 (SN04 NHF) passes through Stoneybank on its way to Queen Margaret College, in Musselburgh, on service 45.

Lothian Buses operate a comprehensive network of night services throughout the week based on some of their day services. Alexander Dennis Enviro400 XLB-bodied Volvo B8L 1107 (SJ19 OYH) is on night service N37 to Silverknowes in Princes Street.

Lothian Buses Alexander Dennis Enviro400 XLB-bodied Volvo B8L 1125 (SJ19 OZD) on night service N16 to Silverknowes at Waverley.

Lothian Buses Skylink compliments Airlink service 100 (Edinburgh City Centre to Edinburgh Airport) with two other services, linking parts of Edinburgh with the airport. Wrightbus Gemini 3-bodied Volvo B5TL 437 (SA15 VTT) is leaving Ocean Terminal along Lindsay Road en route for the Airport on service 200.

Lothian Buses Skylink Wrightbus Gemini 3-bodied Volvo B5TL 507 (SF17 VPG), still wearing an older Airlink livery, is seen at the Fort Kinnaird terminus of service 400.

Lothian Buses Airlink Alexander Dennis Enviro400 XLB-bodied Volvo B8L 1127 (SB19 GLV) is seen at Edinburgh Airport.

Lothian Buses Airlink Alexander Dennis Enviro400 XLB-bodied Volvo B8L 1132 (SB19 GMO), seen leaving Waverley Bridge on a night departure to Edinburgh Airport.

Lothian Buses Airlink Alexander Dennis Enviro400 XLB-bodied Volvo B8L 1140 (SB19 GNK), seen operating an internal site service at the Scottish Vintage Bus Museum open weekend at Lathalmond in 2019.

Lothian Buses Airlink Alexander Dennis Enviro400 XLB-bodied Volvo B8L 1130 (SB19 GME) leaves the Airlink departure point at Edinburgh Airport.

Two generations of Alexander bodywork. Lothian Buses 201 (SN11 EES) is overtaking Alexander Dennis Enviro400 XLB-bodied Volvo B8L 1067 (SJ19 OWA) at the Redford Road terminal point for service 16.

In 2011 the Scottish Government's Green Bus funding allowed Lothian Buses to purchase fifteen Alexander Dennis-bodied Enviro400H diesel-electric hybrid buses. 205 (SN61 BBF) is on service 10 to Bonaly, at St Andrew Square. This is the third livery style worn by the bus since new.

The best way to see Edinburgh is by open-top bus. Lothian Buses Edinburgh Bus Tours generic white-liveried Wright Eclipse Gemini 3-bodied Volvo B5TL 250 (SJ66 LKP) climbs the Mound during the Edinburgh International Festival.

Lothian Buses Edinburgh Bus Tours Wrightbus Gemini-bodied Volvo B9TL 906 (SN08 BXW) is one of two buses that operate the 3 Bridges Tour to Queensferry. Included in the fare is a trip aboard one of the Forth Boat Tours fleet.

Lothian Buses Edinburgh Bus Tours former Go-Ahead London Wrightbus Gemini-bodied Volvo B9TL WVL370 – now 256 (LX60 DXA) – on City Sightseeing duties setting off on a trip around the city from Market Street. This was one of six second-hand vehicles acquired during 2019 to allow an increased frequency following the commencement of a rival Edinburgh tour introduced by First Bus. It was the only fully open-top bus purchased.

Another second-hand Wrightbus Gemini-bodied Volvo B9TL, new to London Centrewest as VN37899 and latterly with London City Tour, Stanwell, entered service with Lothian Buses Edinburgh Bus Tours as 254 (BF60 UUH) and is pictured on the City Sightseeing tour on Hanover Street.

The competition in Edinburgh came in the form of First Scotland East Bright Bus. Their fleet of brightly coloured buses includes Alexander-bodied Dennis Trident 32726 (MXZ 3389) – previously Lothian Buses 526 (V526 ESC). It is seen completing a day's service in Shandwick Place, heading back to its Livingston depot.

In addition to a variety of Dennis Tridents and DAF DB250s, First Bright Bus operate Alexander Dennis-bodied Enviro400 33500 (LK55 KKT). In this photograph it is seen at the impressive setting of Our Dynamic Earth, next to the Scottish Government building at Holyrood.

The fleet of Red Bus Vintage Routemaster Hire in Edinburgh provided vehicles for Voyage des Maires, held at the impressive Gosford Estate in April 2017. Seen in the line-up are former London AEC Routemasters WLT 737, 353 CLT and WLT 875. (Gordon Stirling)

Prentice Westwood, based in West Calder, use Unvi Touring-bodied Mercedes-Benz Atego SN19 BLK on a shuttle bus service to the Glenkinchie Distillery Tour, in East Lothian, which leaves twice daily from the centre of Edinburgh.

While primarily a coach operator, Edinburgh Coachlines, based at Leith, also provide bus service 13 in the capital. YJ62 JWW is an MCV Evolution VDL SB180 bought new and seen at Bellevue on service 13.

Edinburgh Coachlines BX11 GVY, on Frederick Street, carrying out bus duties of service 13 towards Blackhall.

Edinburgh Coachlines Van Hool Alizee T9 PSU 616 on Scottish Citylink service 500 to Glasgow.

As well as service 13 in the capital, Edinburgh Coachlines provide cover on a number of Scottish Citylink services. Irizar i6 Scania K410EB6 YR68 NMF, on Scottish Citylink service 909 to Edinburgh Airport, passes an iconic Spitfire plane.

Waverley Travel operate ADL MMC200 SN66 WJX, which was new to Britannia Parking. The bus is captured passing underneath the impressive RBS Bridge at Gogarburn. (Alistair Train)

Waverley Travel ADL Enviro200 (YX14 RYN), at Clermiston, on tendered local bus service 68 at Corstorphine heading for the Gyle Shopping Centre. (Alistair Train)

Fife and Beyond Edinburgh

New to First London, Scania OmniCity YR61 RSY now resides in Fife with Bay Travel and is pictured on a tendered journey of Kirkcaldy Town service 14. (Chris Cuthill)

Bay Travel own former Yorkshire Coastliner Wrightbus Volvo Gemini B9TL FJ08 BYL. The bus is seen near Kirkcaldy bus station on commercially operated service 18. (Chris Cuthill)

Stagecoach Rennies Plaxton Paragon-bodied Volvo B12M EKZ 469 passes through Musselburgh on a rail replacement service for the Edinburgh to North Berwick train. The bus was new to Yorkshire Traction in 2002 as their 69 (YS02 YXT) before becoming Stagecoach Fife 53029.

Rennies former Stagecoach Selkent Northern Counties Palatine-bodied Volvo Olympian 16423 (N323 HGK), on Market Street in Edinburgh, is seen providing a shuttle to the Edinburgh Marathon. Stagecoach purchased the Rennies operations and the bus ended its days with them still wearing Stagecoach corporate livery. (Chris Cuthill)

Stagecoach Fife ADL Trident Enviro400 19666 (SP60 DPK), in retro 1980s Scottish Bus Group Ayres red and cream Fife Scottish livery, provides a link to the open day at Dunfermline depot celebrating its 100th anniversary in 2018. (Chris Cuthill)

Stagecoach Fife ADL-bodied Enviro300 27532 (SV57 BYM), also in retro Fife Scottish livery, awaits cruise ship passengers at Newhaven in Edinburgh,

Stagecoach Fife Optare Solo 47364 (SP06 FNA) was the third vehicle to wear commemorative livery and is in retro Buzz Bus colours on the 88 Rosyth Europark service. (Chris Cuthill)

Pictured at Wemyssfield, in Kirkcaldy, as it approaches journey's end from Glenrothes, is Stagecoach Fife ADL Enviro300 27134 (SN64 OFX) on the 39B to Kirkcaldy. It carries branding for services between Glenrothes and Kirkcaldy. (Chris Cuthill)

Stagecoach Fife ADL Enviro300 27610 (SP59 CTZ), seen in Dalmeny, on the newly introduced (at that time) service 40A, linking South Queensferry with Edinburgh. Lothian Country now operate this service as the 43. (Chris Cuthill)

An early morning shot of Stagecoach Fife Mini Plaxton Pointer Dennis Dart 34367 (LV52 HGD), in Dunfermline bus station, on service 4 to Blairhall. New to Stagecoach Selkent, the bus moved to Fleet Buzz prior to the purchase of the business by Stagecoach and later transferred to Fife. (Chris Cuthill)

Stagecoach Fife Plaxton Panther LE Volvo B8RLE 54502 (YX18 LHM), with Express City Connect branding, on the X51 arriving at Livingston Centre.

Stagecoach Fife ADL Enviro300 27908 (SN63 VUG) on the 7A arriving at Scone Park and Ride near Perth.

A notably smaller bus in the Stagecoach Fife fleet. 44017 (BV66 GUC) is an Oakley 6 Mercedes Benz Sprinter. It was photographed resting between journeys at Dunfermline Bus Station.

Stagecoach Fife ADL Enviro200 MMC 26004 (YX65 PZD) route branded for the 19/19A service but pictured working route 5.

Taylink 99 branded Stagecoach Fife ADL Enviro200 MMC 26126 (YY18 TGE) at St Andrews Bus Station on service 99A, which links St Andrews, Leuchars and Dundee. (Andrew Chalmers)

Originally new to Stagecoach Yorkshire Traction for National Express work, but now with Stagecoach Fife, is Caetano Levante-bodied Volvo B9R 53733 (BF63 ZRP), working the busy X60 service to Edinburgh.

Stagecoach Fife ADL Enviro400 MMC 11178 (YX19 OUC) performing Edinburgh Marathon shuttle work at Wallyford Toll.

Pictured on Princes Street in Edinburgh, Stagecoach Fife ADL Enviro400 MMC 11184 (YX19 OUJ) is seen on the X60 to Halbeath Park and Ride.

Previously with Stagecoach West Scotland, but seen here with Stagecoach Fife, is Transbus Trident 18020 (SF53 BYU), leaving Wallyford Park and Ride on an Edinburgh Marathon shuttle service.

Stagecoach West Scotland Alexander Dennis Dart IV SLF Enviro300 27815 (SF62 CNO) operates service 101 into Edinburgh and was pictured at Morningside station, heading to West Linton but in Lochside Loop livery.

Seen leaving Edinburgh Airport is Stagecoach Fife ADL Enviro200 MMC 26170 (SN67 WWR), on the branded Jet 747 service for Halbeath Park and Ride.

Stagecoach Fife are starting the first autonomous bus service between Fife and Edinburgh in 2020. A demonstration vehicle was displayed at the 2019 Coach and Bus Show at Birmingham National Exhibition Centre.

Pitlochry

New to Elizabeth Yule in April 2018 is YX18 KUO, one of a pair of ADL Enviro200s, seen on service 87 – the Pitlochry Festival Theatre to Old Straun route.

New to Stagecoach Perth is Alexander-bodied Dennis Dart SLF 37084 (YX14 RYK). The photograph shows the bus arriving at Pitlochry on service 24 but it is branded for 'Muirton on the move'.

West Lothian

Lothian Country required additional buses when it commenced its West Lothian operations in 2017 and acquired four Wright Eclipse 2 Volvo B5LHs from Bullocks of Manchester. These initially ran in all-white livery before being repainted into fleet colours. 594 (LP11 YBB), on a 275 to Livingstone, passes former London Wrightbus Gemini Volvo B9TL 1047 (LXZ 5435), heading into Edinburgh as an X17 at East Mains.

Lothian Country Wrightbus Gemini Volvo B9TL 931 (SN09 CVS), used principally for the 43 service from Edinburgh to South Queensferry, makes an appearance on the 281 to Loganlea at Livingston Centre.

Lothian Country 9201 (SB19 GKE) is one of eight Plaxton Leopard Interurban-bodied Volvo B8Rs purchased for Green Arrow express services and is seen at the Linlithgow terminus of service EX2. The high-spec vehicles feature an impressive nearside disabled ramp entrance for wheelchair users.

Lothian Country Plaxton Leopard Interurban-bodied Volvo B8R 9202 (SB19 GKF), heading through Haymarket on the EX1 to Bathgate. This service was discontinued in November 2019.

Lothian Country Wrightbus Eclipse Urban Volvo B7RLE 119 (SN04 NHK) at the Fauldhouse terminus of the X17.

Lothian Country Wrightbus Eclipse 2 Urban Volvo B7RLE 180 (SN13 BEY) is one of a number of vehicles intended for route X38 between Edinburgh and Linlithgow. It ran unbranded for a short while before the X38 started and is seen on the 287 at St John's Hospital at Howden.

Lothian Country Wrightbus Eclipse 2 Urban Volvo B7RLE 178 (SN13 BEO), showing branding for route X38, leaves Linlithgow bound for Edinburgh city centre.

Generic all-white Wrightbus Eclipse Urban Volvo B7RLE 124 (SN04 NHU) has spent time with both Lothian Buses and Lothian Country. It was whilst with the latter that it was seen on service 281 to Loganlea as it loads up at the Livingston Centre.

Lothian Country have twenty-five of the refurbished former London Metroline Wright Eclipse-bodied Volvo B9TLs. 1029 (LXZ 5414) was captured at St John's Hospital on service 287 to Livingston.

Lothian Country refurbished Wrightbus Gemini-bodied Volvo B9TL 845 (MXZ 1755) was transferred from Lothian Motorcoaches in 2019 and is seen on the 280 bound for Livingston Centre.

Lothian Country Wrightbus Gemini 3-bodied Volvo B5TL 575 (SJ67 MFO) (originally new to the Skylink fleet), seen on holiday by the sea at Blackpool for the 2019 Driver of the Year competition. (Andrew Chalmers)

Lothian Country Wright Eclipse 2 Volvo B5LH (another ex-Bullocks of Manchester acquisition) 591 (LP11 YAX) departs from St Andrew Square, Edinburgh, on the X17 to Fauldhouse. The temporary closure of the normal terminus at Regent Road had necessitated Lothian Country bus services using the alternative departure point.

Another vehicle transferred from the Skylink fleet in 2019 to Lothian Country was Wrightbus Gemini 3-bodied Volvo B5TL 576 (SJ67 MFP), seen turning at the mini roundabout in Regent Road whilst on the X28 to Bathgate. There is an unusual backdrop of some tall cranes during the rebuilding of the St James Centre at the east end of Edinburgh.

Lothian Country refurbished Wrightbus Gemini-bodied Volvo B9TL 849 (MXZ 1759) is another transfer from the Lothian Motorcoaches fleet. It was seen in George Street approaching the Edinburgh terminus in St Andrew Square on the 43 from South Queensferry.

Pictured in the Deans North area of Livingston is First Scotland East 33446 (SN66 WGY) on the 27 to St Andrews Way. (Chris Cuthill)

East Lancs Omnidekka Scania N94UD 36021 (SN05 HWP), in First Scotland East Discovery livery, at Stirling bus station. The bus initially ran in Unilink livery until displaced by new Enviro400 MMCs. (Andrew Chalmers)

Wright Eclipse Gemini-bodied Volvo B7TL 32681 (SN55 HFJ), on service 22, in the two-tone blue livery applied to many First Scotland East and Midland Bluebird vehicles. The bus was pictured on the approach to the Livingston Designer Outlet.

New to First Glasgow, First Scotland East ADL Enviro300 67758 (SN62 ASZ) is seen on service 38 from Edinburgh to Falkirk but is branded in X36 gold livery.

A night-time shot in Edinburgh's Princes Street. First Scotland East (although showing branding for First West Lothian) ADL Enviro400 33449 (SN66 WHB) loads up on service 38 to Benderon.

ADL Enviro400 MMC Hybrid 39305 (SN65 CVM), new to First Scotland East, in special Unilink livery for the service between the university and Stirling city centre.

First Scotland East Wright Eclipse Gemini Volvo B9TL 37266 (SN57 HDG) in the latest version of First livery, at the Livingston Centre, on service 24 to Deans North.

Showing off the latest corporate branding heading into Edinburgh is First Scotland East ADL Enviro400 MMC 33435 (SN66 WGF), on the X23 to Edinburgh.

First Scotland East Enviro400 MMC 33443 (SN66 WGV), displaying the all-pink livery applied to vehicles on service 600, at Edinburgh Airport, heading for Whitburn.

First Scotland East Scania OmniDekka 36013 (SN05 HWL), seen on local service C11 to Aberfoyle in Stirling.

First Scotland East Wright Streetlite Micro-hybrid 63255 (SN65 OKV), seen on service 23, arriving in Edinburgh city centre in the latest route-branded livery.

New to First Eastern Counties, and now with First Scotland East, is ADL Enviro200 45118 (ST09 JPT), in Stirling, on service C30 to Chatton Avenue.

First Scotland East Wright Streetlite 63273 (SN65 OJY) is pictured on Royal Route 38, in Linlithgow, heading to Edinburgh.

First Scotland East ADL Enviro300 67781 (SN62 AYB) passes through Bathgate on service 29 to Broxburn East Mains Industrial Estate.

Originally with First Manchester, and recently transferred from the First Glasgow fleet to First Scotland East, is Wright Eclipse 69183 (MX06 YXP), entering the grounds of St John's Hospital at Howden, on the 27 to Dedridge. In the absence of a working destination screen, the bus carries stickers in the windscreen.

Previously with First Bristol, First Scotland East Streetlite 47445 (SK63 KNU), on service 27, is heading into Livingston station.

First Scotland East Caetano Slimbus-bodied Dennis Dart SLF 43871 (EG52 FFU) was originally new to Connex Transport in Jersey and subsequently transferred around a number of First companies. The bus was pictured at the Livingston Centre on service 27 to Dedridge.

Local Bathgate operator SD Travel used former McGills (new to Hunters of Alloa) ADL Enviro200 YY15 NHZ on their service 31, which runs from Bathgate to Livingston via Linlithgow.

E. & M. Horsburgh provide bus services connecting communities across West Lothian. Optare Solo MX03 YCL is seen at Livingston undertaking the SKY staff bus duty. The bus started life with Accrington Transport.

New to East London as their 18252 (LX04 FYV), E. & M. Horsburgh own Alexander Dennis Trident ALX400 T200 EMH. This view shows the bus on a school hire to Edinburgh Zoo.

Family-run business BlueBus of Shotts provide links between Lanarkshire and West Lothian. Optare Solo YJ67 FZK is seen at Livingston Bus Terminal about to start work on service 701 to Shotts.

Prentice Westwood Mellor-bodied Mercedes Sprinter LO18 TYD is a former demonstrator now owned by the company and pictured in service on route 45 in Linlithgow town centre.